Chapter Introduction

Pictures, photographs, and drawings are important sources of information. This section includes observing and evaluating projects, interpreting information, and following directions.

Extension Activities

📖 Make covers for interesting pictures. Staple the cover on one side of the picture to make a book. Cut a window that reveals a small section of the picture. Ask the students to guess what the rest of the picture looks like. When the guessing session is finished, open the cover. Discuss the clues they found in the small section of the picture that led to their conclusions. Have students make hidden pictures of their own to share with the class.

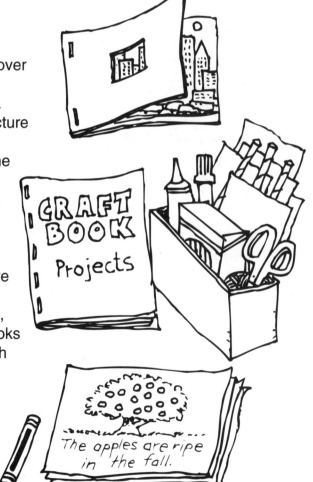

📖 A how-to craft book and a box of construction materials can be given to each group of four or five students as a special Friday afternoon activity. Students select a project and follow the directions, step-by-step, to make the pictured items. The books and boxes can be rotated to a different group each week.

📖 Choose a sequence of pictures. Have students change the information in the pictures to words. Under each picture, write a sentence. (Example: four pictures of an apple tree, one representing each season.)

Name:

Science Fair

1

Study the following three pictures of science fair projects. Rate the projects, first, second, or third by writing a 1, 2, or 3 in each ribbon.

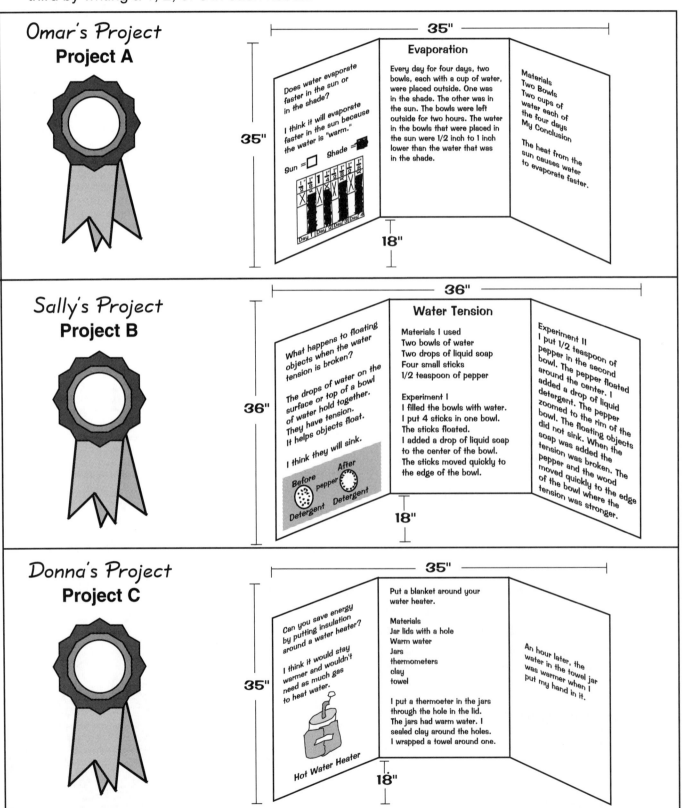

Omar's Project
Project A

35"

35"

Evaporation

Does water evaporate faster in the sun or in the shade?

I think it will evaporate faster in the sun because the water is "warm."

Sun ☐   Shade ■

Every day for four days, two bowls, each with a cup of water, were placed outside. One was in the shade. The other was in the sun. The bowls were left outside for two hours. The water in the bowls that were placed in the sun were 1/2 inch to 1 inch lower than the water that was in the shade.

Materials
Two Bowls
Two cups of water each of the four days
My Conclusion

The heat from the sun causes water to evaporate faster.

18"

Sally's Project
Project B

36"

36"

Water Tension

What happens to floating objects when the water tension is broken?

The drops of water on the surface or top of a bowl of water hold together. They have tension. It helps objects float.

I think they will sink.

Before   After
pepper
Detergent Detergent

Materials I used
Two bowls of water
Two drops of liquid soap
Four small sticks
1/2 teaspoon of pepper

Experiment I
I filled the bowls with water.
I put 4 sticks in one bowl.
The sticks floated.
I added a drop of liquid soap to the center of the bowl.
The sticks moved quickly to the edge of the bowl.

Experiment II
I put 1/2 teaspoon of pepper in the second bowl. The pepper floated around the center. I added a drop of liquid detergent. The pepper zoomed to the rim of the bowl. The floating objects did not sink. When the soap was added the tension was broken. The pepper and the wood moved quickly to the edge of the bowl where the tension was stronger.

18"

Donna's Project
Project C

35"

35"

Can you save energy by putting insulation around a water heater?

I think it would stay warmer and wouldn't need as much gas to heat water.

Hot Water Heater

Put a blanket around your water heater.

Materials
Jar lids with a hole
Warm water
Jars
thermometers
clay
towel

I put a thermoeter in the jars through the hole in the lid. The jars had warm water. I sealed clay around the holes. I wrapped a towel around one.

An hour later, the water in the towel jar was warmer when I put my hand in it.

18"

Name: _____

Science Fair

2

Answer the following questions about the projects shown on Science Sheet 1:
Write the titles of the three science fair projects shown in the pictures on the lines below. Write the conclusion for each project after the title. Hint: Perhaps the students forgot their title or conclusion.

Omar's Project   **Project A**

Title: _____

Conclusion: _____

Sally's Project   **Project B**

Title: _____

Conclusion: _____

Donna's Project   **Project C**

Title: _____

Conclusion: _____

Give out 1st, 2nd, and 3rd prize. Write the numbers inside the ribbons on sheet 1. Now read the science fair rules.

Science Fair Rules

1. The display cannot be larger than 18 inches deep and 35 inches long and high. It can be smaller. If the display does not stand by itself, it will be disqualified.
2. The display must state a problem, include a student guess about the outcome of the project, and list the procedure that was followed. Observations are recorded.
3. The conclusion must be clearly stated.
4. The information must be accurate.

Did your ratings change? _____

Explain your answer. _____

_____

_____

Name:

Track and Field

Students from Anderson and Taylor High Schools are competing in a track meet. Study the pictures and information below and fill in the missing information on sheets 1 and 2. Then answer the questions on sheet 3.

13 seconds 12 seconds 11.5 seconds 11.8 seconds 11 seconds 14 seconds

100 Yard Dash

Player	Number	School	Place
Brenner	15	Taylor	____
Garcia	26	Taylor	____
Welsh	31	Anderson	____
Rashad	12	Taylor	____
Washington	18	Anderson	____
Fernandes	22	Anderson	____

6 feet 5 feet 3 feet 4 feet 6 inches 3 feet 6 inches 4 feet

High Jump

Player	Number	School	Place
Evans	____	Taylor	____
Macpherson	____	Taylor	____
Washington	____	Anderson	____
Yee	____	Taylor	____
Nguyen	____	Anderson	____
Blum	____	Anderson	____

Name:

Track and Field

2

Record the points and missing information on the score sheets.

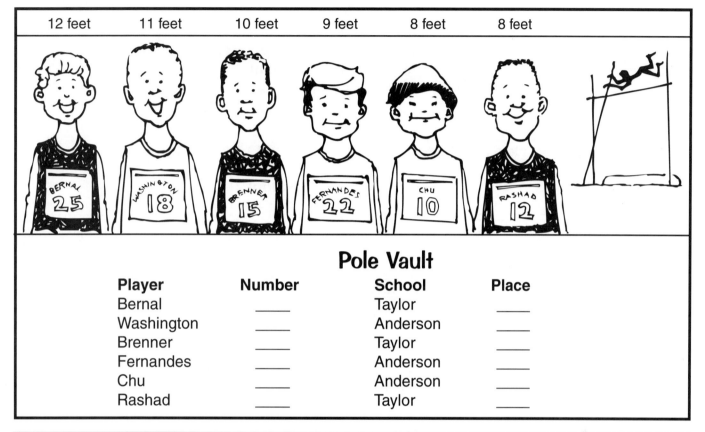

12 feet	11 feet	10 feet	9 feet	8 feet	8 feet

BERNAL 25 · WASHINGTON 18 · BRENNER 15 · FERNANDES 22 · CHU 10 · RASHAD 12

Pole Vault

Player	Number	School	Place
Bernal	_____	Taylor	_____
Washington	_____	Anderson	_____
Brenner	_____	Taylor	_____
Fernandes	_____	Anderson	_____
Chu	_____	Anderson	_____
Rashad	_____	Taylor	_____

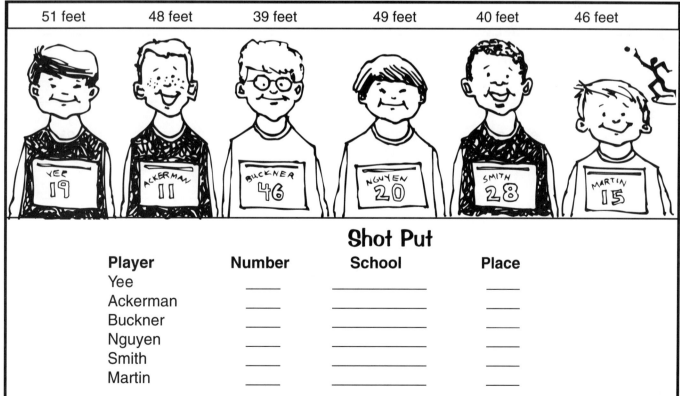

51 feet	48 feet	39 feet	49 feet	40 feet	46 feet

YEE 19 · ACKERMAN 11 · BUCKNER 46 · NGUYEN 20 · SMITH 28 · MARTIN 15

Shot Put

Player	Number	School	Place
Yee	_____	_____	_____
Ackerman	_____	_____	_____
Buckner	_____	_____	_____
Nguyen	_____	_____	_____
Smith	_____	_____	_____
Martin	_____	_____	_____

Name: _____

Track and Field

In this meet, points were gained for first, second, and third place finishes. Record the points gained in the boxes below.

- First place earns **5 points.**
- Second place earns **3 points.**
- Third place earns **1 point.**
- The other athletes in the event earn no points.
- Tally the wins and points for each school.

Anderson High School

1st place wins	1st place points

2nd place wins	2nd place points

3rd place wins	3rd place points

	Total points

Taylor High School

1st place wins	1st place points

2nd place wins	2nd place points

3rd place wins	3rd place points

	Total points

1. Who won the track meet? By how many points?

_____

2. Which athletes competed in more than one event?   List their names after the name of their school.

Anderson _____

Taylor _____

3. Which athlete earned the most points? _____

How many points? _____

4. Which event would you like to compete in? _____

Why? _____

Name:

Pinwheel

1

Follow the steps below to make an interesting wind machine.

Materials:

- construction paper 6" X 6" (15 cm) square
- new pencil with eraser
- pushpin
- ruler
- crayons or markers
- tape

Directions:

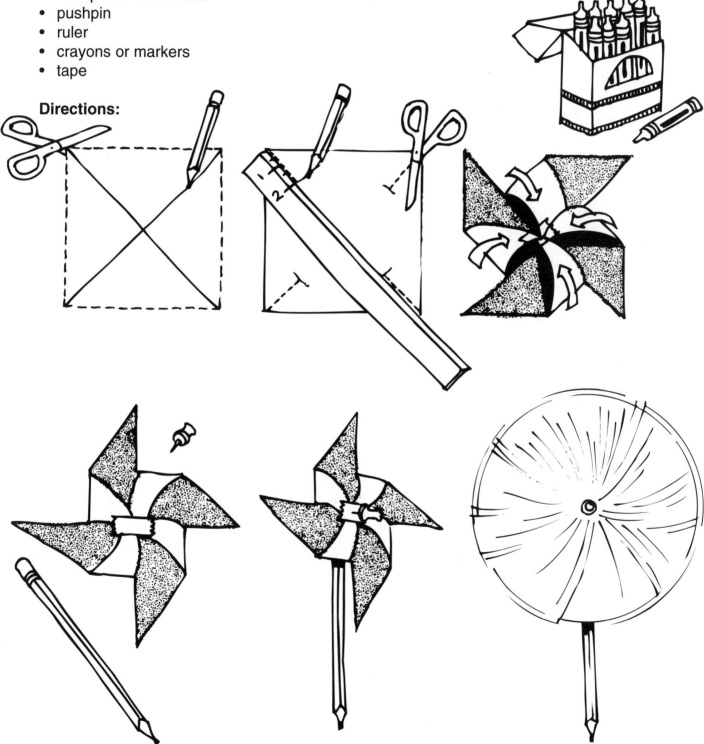

Following Directions

Chapter Introduction

Students need to practice reading and following directions. Reading how to assemble objects, filling out forms, and following game directions challenge young readers. This section of *Survival Reading Skills* introduces direction-following skills.

Extension Activities

Make copies of the order form on page 10. Bring in examples of various catalogs. Give pairs of students catalogs and have them write out an order for four items, or you can give them a set amount of money to spend.

Discuss vocabulary words in this section. Students may not be familiar with the words: merchandise, refund, shipping and handling charges, money order.

Write the directions for the last 15 minutes of the school day on the board. List the times by which tasks must be finished. Include everything from cleaning up, homework information, and what they need to do before they are dismissed. Add a point system or small incentive for completing the tasks quietly.

Write out the directions for an art project that require several steps to finish. Have the students follow the directions and complete the project on their own.

Name:

In-Line Skates

There are many ways to shop. Some stores send out catalogs so you can shop at home. When you order from a catalog, it's important to read carefully and think about the following things:

- Is the product what you really want to buy?
- Does the quality of the product ensure it will it last a long time?
- Is it the right size?
- Is the price less than the same item in the store, including the shipping and handling charges?

It is time to go shopping with a friend! On these three pages you will help "a friend" order skates and then evaluate his order.

Jeffrey A. O'Brien lives with his parents in Oakville, California (zip code 97655). He has been saving money to buy in-line skates. His parents said he had to wait until he had enough money for a helmet and protective pads, too. This will ensure his safety as he's skating near his house at 44 Washington Avenue. This month he received $40 for his birthday. Now, with the money he has saved, he has $139.00. He thinks it's enough for medium-priced skates. His shoe size is 7 1/2. He has called you to come over and help him fill out the order form. You telephoned him back at (523) 787-3344 to say you would be right there.

Jeffrey decided to order the following items:

Safe Landing Protective Pack

#L69398
One size, adjustable 6 piece set.
Knee, elbow, and wrist pads.
Foam inner lining with hard plastic
outside covers for the knees and
elbows.
Weight: 2.20 lbs.

Price $18.69

Dial-a-Size Helmet

#M89356
Adjustable. Fits most adults
Red, blue, or silver.
Safety helmet suitable for
most sports except
motorcycling. Air vents.
Weight: 2.80 lbs.
.

Price:$41.20

Lightning In-Line Skates

#C97321
One-piece construction. Vented
polyurethane boot with comfort
insoles. Y class bearings and
medium-hard wheels. Long-lasting,
with a feel for the road.
Adult sizes 6, 7, 8, 9, 10, 11, 12.
Protective pack included. Rink safe.
Weight: 8 lbs.

Price: $51.98

Name:

In-Line Skates

Fill in the following order form. Be careful to read and follow all the directions.

Best Buy Catalog

Name: First   Middle Initial   Last   Area Code   Telephone

Address   City   State   Zip Code

Item	Catalog Number	Weight	Size	Color	Price
1					
2					
3					
4					

Total price of order: _____

Sales tax (8%): _____

Total weight: _____ Shipping and handling: _____

Amount owed: _____

Ordering Information
Women and girls should order skates two sizes smaller than their regular shoe size. Skates are not available in half sizes. Order the next higher size if you need a half-size. Enclose a check or money order that includes the shipping and handling charges and sales tax for your state.

Refunds
If you are not satisfied with your purchase, you may return the order. Merchandise must be returned within thirty days after receipt. Postage, shipping and handling charges, and sales tax will be refunded if the merchandise has not been damaged by the customer. If you are due a refund, a separate check will be mailed to you within thirty days after the store receives the returned merchandise.

Shipping Charges

Weight	Delivery Charges
0-4.9 lbs.	$6.00
5-9.9 lbs.	$8.00
10-19.9 lbs.	$12.50
20-34.9 lbs.	$15.00

For each additional pound, add 25¢. Weights are listed by tenths of a pound. Total the weight for the entire order before adding the shipping and handling charges.

Following Directions

Name: _____

In-Line Skates

3

After filling out the catalog order form, answer the following questions about Jeffrey's order.

1. Why will Jeffrey be surprised when he receives his order?

_____

_____

_____

2. What can Jeffrey do to correct the mistake he made? Read the section on **Refunds** before you write your answer.

_____

_____

_____

3. What is the amount of the refund Jeffrey will receive? Don't forget to include any extra money he paid for shipping and handling, sales tax, and $3.69 he paid for postage to return the merchandise. Show all your work here.

4. How long will Jeffrey need to wait for his refund?

_____

5. What could Jeffrey have done differently so that he would not have to go to the trouble of returning something?

_____

6. Have you ever ordered anything from a catalog? _____

If yes, what was the last thing you ordered? _____

Name:

Put It Together

1

Many items bought in the store have to be assembled, or put together, when you bring them home. The first step in assembling a bookcase, tool, or toy is to read the directions and then make sure all the parts listed are in the package. Next, see what tools you will need to put the item together. Set up a tool box. Put all the tools you will need in the box.

Margaret loves to read! She bought a new bookcase for her room. It was unassembled. Complete sheet 2, then follow the instructions on sheets 3 and 4 to help Margaret assemble her bookcase.

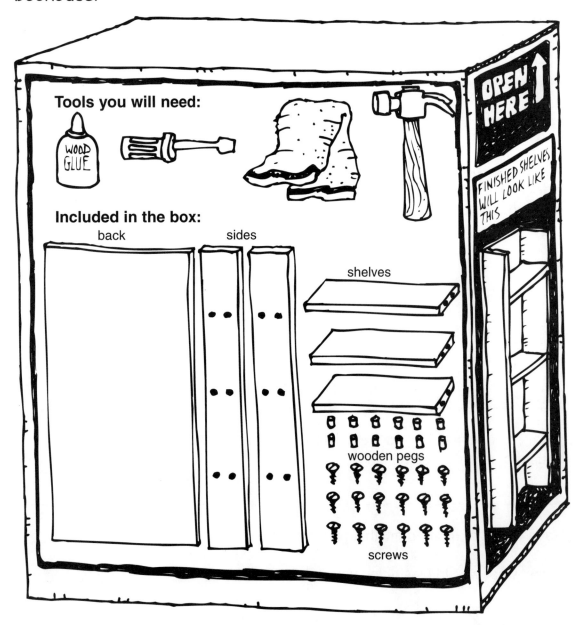

12

Name: _____

Put It Together

2

1. List four steps Margaret should follow before she begins to put the bookcase together:

First _____

Then _____

Next _____

Then _____

2. List the tools needed to put the bookcase together:

_____   _____

_____   _____

3. List all the parts and how many of each are included for building the bookcase.

Number   **Name**

_____   _____

_____   _____

_____   _____

_____   _____

_____   _____

4. Draw a picture in the box of what you think the bookcase wil look like after it is assembled and Margaret has filled it.

Name:

Put It Together

3

Read the directions for assembling the bookcase carefully. Cut the pictures from the bottom of sheets 3 and 4 and paste each illustration in the box next to the correct step.

1. Flatten the cardboard box that the bookcase came in and use it to cover the floor where you are working. It will keep glue off the floor.

paste here

2. Begin with the bottom shelf and the left side of the bookcase. Set the boards flat on the cardboard. Fill the holes on one end of the shelf with glue. Fill the two holes at the bottom of the side board with glue.

paste here

3. Place two pegs in the two glued holes on the side board. Fasten the other ends of the pegs to the glued holes in the shelf. With the hammer, gently tap the top edge of the shelf until the pegs are tightly locked into the side board. There should be no space between the two boards. Wipe off the excess glue.

paste here

4. Fasten the other two shelves the same way.

paste here

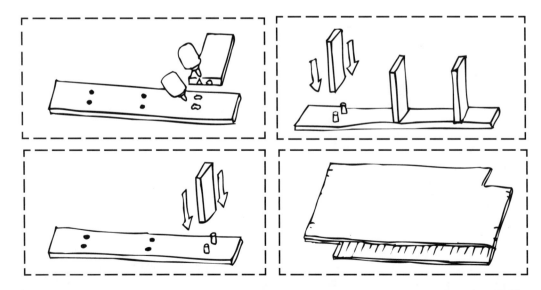

Name:

Put It Together

5. When all three shelves are tight and the glue is set, fill all the holes on the open side of the shelves with glue. Fill the holes in the right side board with glue. Place one end of the pegs in the holes in the three shelves. Line up the holes on the right side of the board that is facing up with the shelf pegs and insert the pegs in the holes.

paste here

6. Carefully set a towel over the side board. Gently pound the side board, moving from one peg to another, until there is no space between the shelves and the side boards.

paste here

7. When the glue is set, place the bookcase face down on the cardboard. Put the two top corner screws into the pre-drilled holes in the bookcase back. Be sure they are lined-up with the holes in the bookcase. Tighten the screws. Fasten the bottom screws next.

paste here

8. Attach the remaining screws for a sturdy bookcase.

paste here

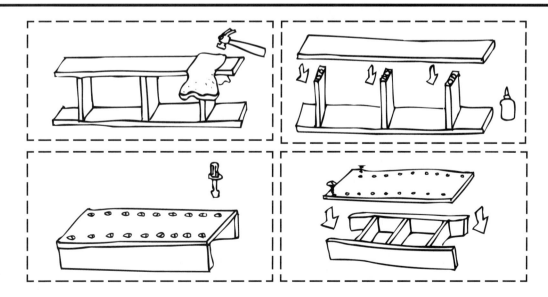

Following Directions

Name:

Just for Fun

1

Following directions will help you solve many picture and word puzzles. Complete the instructions below to fill in the letters for this wise Chinese proverb.

```
··              ··—           ··                          ·
—  —    — — —    — — — —    — —    — — — —
1  2    3 4 5    6 7 8 9   10 11   12 13 14 15
·—            ··—        ·— ··          ·—
—    — — — — — — — — — ,   — — — — —
16   17 18 19 20 21 22 23 24   25 26 27 28 29
·—  ·—      ·—        ·                    ·
— — — —    —      — — —      — — — — — —
30 31 32 33  34    35 36 37    38 39 40 41 42 43
·—      ·—
— — —    —      — — — — — .
44 45    46     47 48 49 50
```

1. The last word in this saying is a word that describes seconds, minutes, and hours.

2. There are four more "T"s in this saying. Write the letter "T" above the following numbers: 10, 21, 39, 45.

3. There are 5 "O"s in this saying. "O" is the second letter in words two, four, five, and seven. It is the third letter in the fourth word from the end.

4. Morse code is a system of dots and dashes that represents letters. Use the code to fill in the vowels in the proverb.

```
A   ·—
E   ·
I   ··
U   ··—
```

5. There are three "Y"s in this proverb. The first one is the first letter of the second word. The other two are at the end of the eighth and ninth words.

6. Write the letter "W" over numbers 6, 31, and 37.

7. The first letter of the fifth and seventh words is the third letter of the last word in the proverb.

©1996 by Evan-Moor Corp.   16   Survival Reading Skills EMC 573

Name:

Just for Fun

7. There are two letter "R"s next to each other in the eighth word.

8. The third word rhymes with "fish."

9. The eleventh word means "not many."

10. The twelfth word begins and ends with "S."

11. The eighth word means "to transport something."

12. Three "N"s, two "F"s, one "V", and one "C" are missing.
Write them in the correct spaces.

You've solved the puzzle! In your own words, write what the proverb means:

_____

_____

_____

_____

"Rome wasn't built in a day" is another well-known saying that is similar to the mystery proverb. How are the two proverbs alike?

_____

_____

_____

_____

_____

Challenge
Work in pairs to write mystery messages. Make up a code. See if your classmates can follow your directions and discover the message.

Knot Work

Directions can help someone build a house, operate a car, or fix a television set. You can learn to make things by reading the directions in hobby and craft books. The following directions will show you how to tie a special kind of knot.

Directions: Put the letter of each picture in the box next to the matching directions.

1. The Sheet Bend knots two pieces of rope together. It is a good knot to use when you need to tie ropes that are not the same thickness.

2. Hold one of the ropes with one hand. Wrap the free end of the rope around the hand holding the rope.

3. Slip your fingers out of the rope. Set the loop on a flat surface. The loose end of the string that goes to the right must be on the underneath side of the loop.

4. Pick up the other piece of rope with the other hand. Pull one end of the rope under the bottom of the loop and out over the top of the loop.

5. The end of this rope goes underneath the right end of the other rope above the loop.

6. Bring the rope you pulled through the loop, back down through the loop — a U-turn.

7. Pull on both ends of the U-Turn rope and both top end of the other rope to tie the knot.

Now try to tie a sheet bend knot. Books on knot tying are available. Practice tying a variety of knots. Amaze your friends and family.

Forms and Applications

Chapter Introduction

When you want to go to camp, enter a drawing to win a prize, apply for a job, or sign up for a library card, you need to read directions and fill out forms and applications.

It's important that students read all the information and questions before they begin to write. Stress that their answers should be filled in neatly or typed. In this section of *Survival Reading Skills,* students will fill out applications and write a letter to apply for work. These are life skills necessary for all students to have.

📖 Introduce all vocabulary you feel your students may not know. This may include: application, resident, receipt, merchandise, physical limitations, rebate, and entry blank.

📖 Before beginning *Camp Goodtimes,* decide whether forms will actually be sent home to obtain parent signatures and emergency information. Discuss the fact that on many applications there are questions that are optional. Questions about religion and race are optional. It would be against the law to discriminate, or turn down your application, because of your race or religion.

📖 Discuss the fact that students are minors and what that means. Many forms require a parent or guardian's signature and proof that the student lives where he or she lives. Discuss the purpose for this.

📖 Discuss what a Social Security number is, why you need one, and where you can obtain one. All students should have a number. You might want to get some applications from your local Social Security office and fill them out as a class activity.

📖 Work permits are discussed. Contact your local employment agency to find information regarding work permits to pass on to your students.

         Survival Reading Skills EMC 573

Name:

Working in the School Store

You have decided to apply to work at lunchtime in the school store. You need to fill out the application and write a letter explaining why you want to work in the store.

Application to Work in the School Store

Name_____

Grade _____   Room Number _____

Teacher's Name _____

Circle days you are able to work: M   T   W   TH   F

1. I will be willing to work as a substitute in the store when other helpers are absent.
     Yes   **No**

2. My citizenship grade was satisfactory for the last two months of school.
     Yes   **No**

3. I received passing grades for all my subjects on the last report card.
     Yes   **No**

If your teacher signs this application, you may apply to work in the store even if the answer to the last question is No.

_____ has my permission to work in the school store.

_____
(Teacher's Signature)

- If selected to work in the store for three months, I will leave my classroom twenty minutes early to eat my lunch on the one day I am working.
- I will report for work on time.
- I will return to class twenty minutes after the store closes.
- I will be respectful to customers and other workers in the store.
- I will do my best to follow directions and complete my duties.
- I will help put away the merchandise and fill out the records for the sales and money received that day.
- I understand I need to make up any work I miss when I am not in my classroom.

Your Signature: _____

Name:

Working in the School Store

2

Answer the following questions about the application.

1. How long will each person work in the store?

_____

2. How many days a week will each person work?

_____

3. What will happen if someone is absent?

_____

4. What duties will students working in the store have?

_____

_____

_____

_____

5. How much time will each student worker miss from the classroom each week?

_____

6. In what ways can a store worker be respectful to customers? _____

_____

7. Joe buys 3 pencils that are $.25 each, a book cover for $ .75, 2 erasers that are $ .30 each, and an apple for snack that is $ .50. How much change will you give him back from the $5.00 bill he gave you? Show all your work below.

Name:

Working in the School Store

On another paper, write a letter explaining why you want to work in the school store. When you write the letter, use this guide for a business letter.

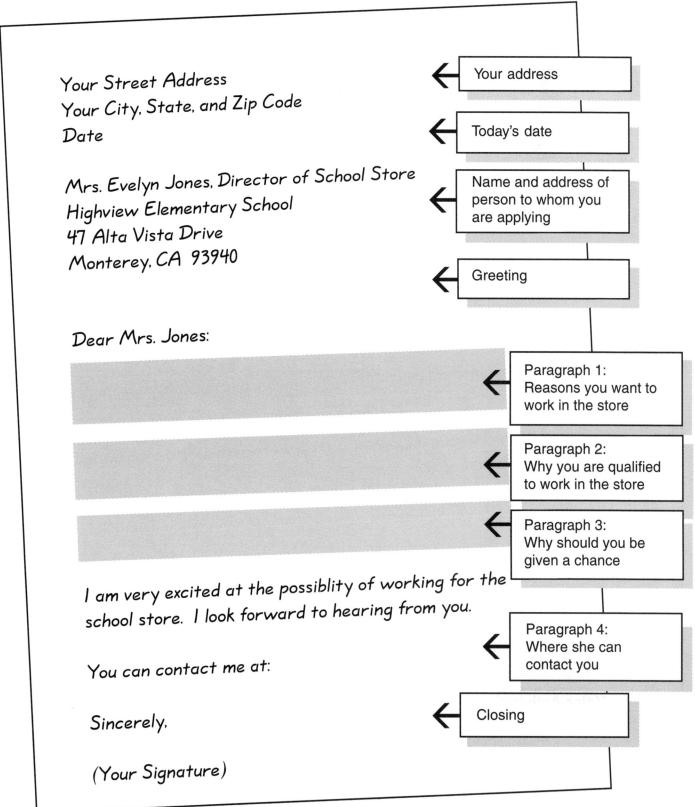

Your Street Address
Your City, State, and Zip Code
Date

Mrs. Evelyn Jones, Director of School Store
Highview Elementary School
47 Alta Vista Drive
Monterey, CA 93940

Dear Mrs. Jones:

I am very excited at the possiblity of working for the school store. I look forward to hearing from you.

You can contact me at:

Sincerely,

(Your Signature)

← Your address

← Today's date

← Name and address of person to whom you are applying

← Greeting

← Paragraph 1: Reasons you want to work in the store

← Paragraph 2: Why you are qualified to work in the store

← Paragraph 3: Why should you be given a chance

← Paragraph 4: Where she can contact you

← Closing

Forms and
Applications

Name:

Camp Goodtimes

1

Application for

Summer Camp

Section 1 - Personal Information

_____

First Name   Middle Initial   Last Name

_____

Address   City   State   Zip Code

_____

Telephone

_____

Date of Birth   Grade   School

Circle: Male   Female

Session You Wish to Attend:

July 5 - July 19   July 21 - August 6   August 8 - August 22

Major Activity:

Sports and Swimming   Computers   Art and Music

Note: Campers will have many outdoor activities as well as the section they have chosen.

©1996 by Evan-Moor Corp.   23   Survival Reading Skills EMC 573

Name:

Camp Goodtimes

Section 2 - Emergency Information

1. List any activities the camper cannot participate in _____

2. List allergies, physical limitations _____

3. List any medications the camper needs to take_____

4. Parent/Guardian's Name_____

_____
Address   City   State   Zip Code

5. Work Telephone _____

6. Home Telephone _____

7. Emergency Contacts
List two people the camp can contact if the parent/guardian is not available.

A. Name_____

Telephone _____

Relationship _____

B. Name_____

Telephone _____

Relationship _____

8. Persons who may pick up the camper beside the parent:

_____

Anyone picking up the child at camp must be listed on this application. Picture identification is required. Please notify the camp director if the camper will be going home with someone other than the parent.

Parent or Guardian's Signature _____ Date _____

Name:

Camp Goodtimes

Section 3 - Optional Information

The answers are for statistical information only.

Ethnic/race: Black   Hispanic   White   Native American

                Asian   Other _____

Religion _____

Number of children in the family _____

This application must be mailed by May 1.

Answer the following questions about the application.

1. What section of the application can be left blank?

_____

2. Why isn't it necessary to fill in that information?

_____

3. List three safety procedures the camp has to protect the campers.

_____

_____

_____

4. Why does the application have questions about health and medication?

_____

5. Who must sign the application?

_____

6. By what date should the application be mailed?

_____

Applying for a Job

1

Martin Palma will celebrate his eighteenth birthday on the first day of July. He graduates from Oneida City High School on June 15th. Martin needs to earn money to help pay for college expenses in the fall. Last summer he worked mowing and trimming lawns. This summer he wants to work full time at Baker's Food Market. He filled out the application on April 3rd. Martin wants to begin work the week after he graduates. He would like to be a check-out clerk, bag groceries, stock shelves, or help in the fresh produce department. Since the college he will go to is nearby, he plans to work one day on the weekends during the school year. Read Martin's job application carefully. Sheet 2 will ask you questions about it.

Baker's Food Market

	Martin	*Antonio*	*Palma*
1. Print full name:	Last Name	First Name	Middle Name

	294 Park Avenue	*Oneida*		*42765*
2. Address:	Number and Street	City	State	Zip Code

443-2214	*739-27-6661*
3. Telephone Number	Social Security Number

4. Education: ___*Oneida City*___ High School   Did you graduate? (Yes)   No

College: *Appleton University*   Are you a student? (Yes)   No

5. Work Experience: *Any job available*

6. For what job are you applying? *Gardening, mowing lawns*

7. When can you work? (Circle the times below.)
- (Full time)
- (Part time)
- (After school)
- (Weekends)

8. When can you begin work? *June 22*

If you are under 18 years of age, you must attach a work permit. Check here if attached. ☐

Applying for a Job

Martin made errors when he filled out the application. Go over the application carefully and circle as many as you can find. List them here:

1. _____

2. _____

3. _____

4. _____

5. _____

6. _____

7. _____

Answer the following questions about the application:

1. Since Martin was almost 18 years old, he did not attach a work permit, but he should have. When could he start work without the permit?

_____

2. How should Martin write his name on the application form?

_____

3. Write your name in the same order.

_____

4. Martin wants full-time summer work and part-time work during the following school year. Since there wasn't room to explain on the form, Martin needs to write an explanation. On the lines below, write the explanation for Martin.

_____

_____

_____

_____

Name: _____

Applying for a Library Card

1

When applying for a library card, you will need a parent or guardian's signature and proof that your family lives in the city served by the library. A rent receipt, a driver's license, or an electric bill are some of the items that could be used to prove where your family lives.

Fill out the following application for a library card.

Jackson County Library

Please Print

Name _____

              (Last)   (First)   (Middle Initial)

Mailing Address

_____

(Street Address or P.O. Box)

_____

    (City)   (State)   (Zip Code)

Home Address if Different from Mailing Address

_____

(Address)   (City)   (State)   (Zip Code)

If you have moved during the last two years, or changed your name, please list your previous address or name below.

Previous Name _____

Previous Address _____

I have had a County Library Card before. (Circle)   Yes   No

I agree to follow all the library rules. I will pay promptly any library fines for lost or damaged books. I will be responsible for all materials checked out with my card.

_____

(Signature)

If you are under age 14, your parent or legal guardian must sign this application.

_____

(Signature of Parent or Guardian)

Contests, Rebates, and Advertisements

Chapter Introduction

Contests, product rebates, and advertisements all require careful reading. Lack of comprehension may mean not complying with all the rules, not getting a refund, or buying a product that doesn't fulfill expectations.

Introduce the words: promote, endorse, techniques, persuade, and convince.

Extension Activities

Many stores offer in-house entry blanks. Collect as many samples as you can and bring them to your students. Have them read all the fine print to find out what exactly they need to do and what they get.

Rebates comes in all forms and sizes. Find a rebate offer and share it with your students. Have them help you list all the steps involved in receiving that rebate— from purchasing the product, to keeping the receipt, to addressing the envelope, and then waiting for the designated time.

Discuss what a proof-of-purchase seal is and where it can be found. Also, talk about its use and importance.

Collect lots of advertisements from magazines, newspapers, and "junk" mail. Tape some TV ads. Evaluate the techniques used to convince people to buy.

Name: _____

The Winning Ticket

1

When you fill out forms to win prizes, you need to follow directions carefully. Read the directions to fill out the entry blank on sheet 1. Answer the question about it on sheet 2.

Entry Blank

Win a new bicycle, a computer, or a movie for your home entertainment center! There are hundreds of prizes including free movie-rental certificates. No purchase necessary. Just fill out this entry blank and deposit it in the entry blank box at *Hazel's Movie Stop*. One entry blank per person. Entry blanks must be deposited by March 1. Winning entry blanks will be drawn on March. You do not need to be present to win. To help us serve our customers, answer the three questions at the bottom of the entry blank and turn them in at the counter. You'll receive a certificate for a free candy bar when you rent your next movie.

Hazel's Movie Stop

_____
Name

_____
Address

_____
Telephone Number

Cut here

1. About how many movies do you rent each month?_____

2. Circle the three movies you enjoy the most?   (comedys, musicals, cartoons, children's movies, westerns, drama, action)

3. What can Hazel's do to improve service for customers?

_____

Name: _____

The Winning Ticket

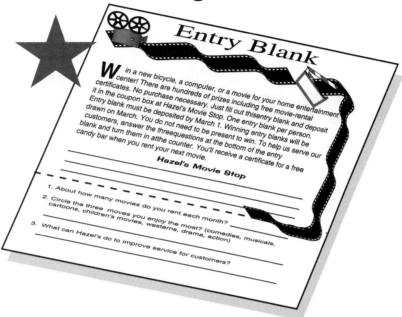

Entry Blank

Win a new bicycle, a computer, or a movie for your home entertainment center! There are hundreds of prizes including free movie-rental certificates. No purchase necessary. Just fill out this entry blank and deposit it in the coupon box at Hazel's Movie Stop. One entry blank per person. Entry blank must be deposited by March 1. Winning entry blanks will be drawn on March. You do not need to be present to win. To help us serve our customers, answer the three questions at the bottom of the entry blank and turn them in at the counter. You'll receive a certificate for a free candy bar when you rent your next movie.

Hazel's Movie Stop

1. About how many movies do you rent each month?
2. Circle the three moves you enjoy the most? (comedies, musicals, cartoons, children's movies, westerns, drama, action)
3. What can Hazel's do to improve service for customers?

---

1. By what date must the entry blanks be in the box? _____

2. Do you have to be present to win? _____

3. What three things do you have to do before you receive the gift?

_____

_____

_____

4. How many prizes will be awarded?

_____

5. Rewrite the sentence about the prizes so customers will know the exact number of prizes Hazel's will give away. You decide the number.

_____

_____

6. What will you receive if you fill out the questionnaire at the bottom of the entry blank? _____

Name:

Sending for a Rebate

When you fill out a form to receive a rebate (money back), you need to follow directions carefully. Read the directions for sending for a rebate for *Fireball Red-Hot, Chewy Gum Balls.*

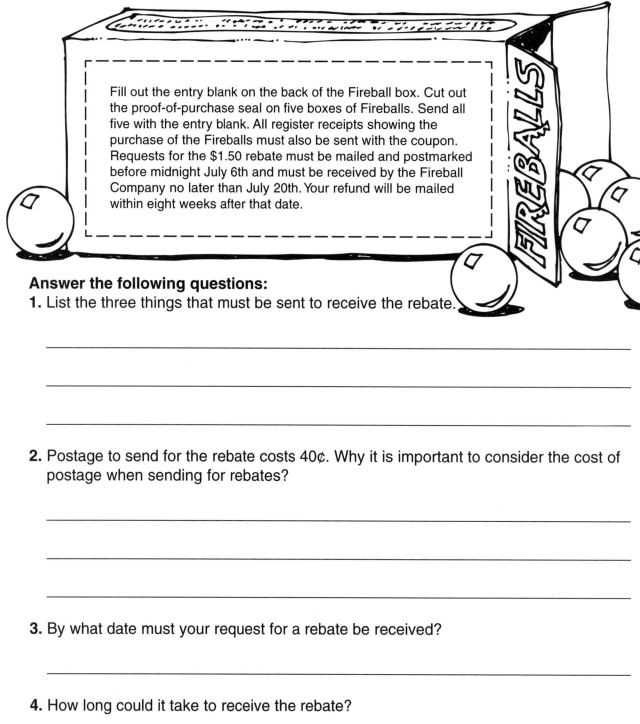

Fill out the entry blank on the back of the Fireball box. Cut out the proof-of-purchase seal on five boxes of Fireballs. Send all five with the entry blank. All register receipts showing the purchase of the Fireballs must also be sent with the coupon. Requests for the $1.50 rebate must be mailed and postmarked before midnight July 6th and must be received by the Fireball Company no later than July 20th. Your refund will be mailed within eight weeks after that date.

Answer the following questions:

1. List the three things that must be sent to receive the rebate.

_____

_____

_____

2. Postage to send for the rebate costs 40¢. Why it is important to consider the cost of postage when sending for rebates?

_____

_____

_____

3. By what date must your request for a rebate be received?

_____

4. How long could it take to receive the rebate?

_____

Name:

Buy! Buy! Buy!

1

Advertisers use different techniques to try to convince people that they really need a product. Here are five such techniques.

1 Join the Crowd
Some advertisements make you think that large numbers of people use the product. They try to convince you to join the crowd and buy it too. They may use percentages and say that 85% or 95% of all the people surveyed use the product. Of course, the advertisement may not let you know who these people are or how often they use the product.

2 Ask an Expert
Experts interviewed in an ad say it's a great product. For example, a doctor says she recommends a headache medicine for her patients. These people are paid to advertise and endorse (associate their name with) the product. The advertisement doesn't say if they use other products as well.

3 Be the Best
If a famous basketball player says he plays better when he wears Brand X athletic shoes, other people will buy the shoes so they can be better athletes and win more basketball games. Most famous people are paid large amounts of money to advertise a product.

4 Over and Over Again
 An advertisement may repeat the brand name many times so people will think of that name when they go to the store. For example, Sudsy Soap TV advertisements show that clothes washed in Sudsy are bright and clean. They repeat the word Sudsy in every sentence. When viewers shop, they'll remember the name Sudsy.

5 Superb, Marvelous, and Fantastic
Some ads use descriptive words and pictures to convince people that the products will improve people's lives or the way they feel. The ad may show a beautiful tropical sunset on an island beach. Words like *unforgettable*, *breathtaking*, *peaceful*, and *heavenly* are used with the picture to convince travelers to vacation on the island. Negative words, words that make you uncomfortable, can be used to show that people who don't use a product will be very unhappy. For example, you can have tired, aching feet that make you feel miserable if you don't wear Comfy Slippers when you do your homework.

Name:

Buy! Buy! Buy!

2

Read the following advertisements. Which of the five techniques did the advertisers use to sell the product? Write the number of the technique in the circle at the top left of each advertisement.

○ **FLUFFY**

Fluffy is a winner. She has a room filled with trophies and blue ribbons to prove it. She's been named top cat at cat shows all over the country. To keep her prize-winning form, Fluffy eats top quality *Super Cat.* **The ingredients in** *Super Cat* **keep Fluffy healthy and content. Feed your cat** *Super Cat,* **and watch your feline friend develop winning ways like Fluffy.**

 ○ SAM'S PIZZA!!!

Come to Sam's Pizza for a mouthwatering treat. Only at Sam's Pizza can you sink your teeth into layer after layer of creamy cheeses topped with tomatoes and garden vegetables. Sam's Pizza's Vegetarian Delight is spread over a crunchy Italian crust. Right now Sam's Pizza has a special you won't want to miss—two giant-size pizzas for the price of one! So tonight, let Sam's Pizza cook, set the table, and wash the dishes. Call Sam's Pizza and reserve a table. Sam's Pizza has banquet rooms big enough for the whole family. Bring your cousins, uncles, aunts, and grandparents to Sam's.

 ○ **SNEAKERS**

Sneakers **outsells all other brands of sports shoes. Three out of four people surveyed chose** *Sneakers* **over other brands. For walking, jogging, aerobics, or tennis,** *Sneakers* **has the style you need. Be part of the team. Go** *Sneakers!*

○

GLOW
Toothpaste

Dr. Ana Lee recommends *Glow Toothpaste.* "*Glow* keeps me smiling. I recommend it for its fresh-mint flavor and its decay-fighting ingredients. There's always a tube of *Glow* in my medicine cabinet at home."

Now it's your turn!
Write a list of words about your favorite food that would make other people want to eat that food. Use some of those words to fill in the blanks for the following advertisement.

○ _____"Yummy Bar"

When you bite into a _____ Yummy Bar, close your eyes and smell the _____ chocolate coating and cherry caramel filling. Its _____ aroma will get you ready for Yummy's _____ taste. Chew slowly and savor each _____ bite. _____!
You deserve a _____ Yummy break every day.

Directions and Diagrams, Labels and Signs

Chapter Introduction

Before doing *What's for Breakfast?* and *Lunch Time,* you may need to provide background information so that students understand nutritional terms (sodium, cholesterol, etc.) and have criteria for determining healthy foods (lower fat, sugar, sodium, cholesterol; high fiber; vitamins and minerals).

In this section of Survival Reading Skills, students will practice programming a VCR, following the directions for a recipe, reading food labels on cereal boxes, and locating items in a store.

Extension Activities

📖 Ask students to bring two labeled articles of clothing to school. Make a large chart with columns labeled *Clothing Item*, *Size*, *Country*, *Material*, *Care*. Ask the students to list the information about the clothing they brought. As a class, summarize and make generalizations about the information.

📖 Have students bring in samples of their favorite recipe along with the printed recipe. They can give a step-by-step report of how the item was prepared without actually doing the cooking. Copies of the recipes can be made for the other students and everyone can enjoy a sample taste.

Name:

Take a Look

1

There are many different remote controls for VCRs. It's important to read the directions for any remote control before you turn it on.

Look at the remote control diagram and read the instructions written on the page.

Set the Clock
Press the PROG button. When the program menu comes on, press 3 for clock. Use the numbers on the remote control to set the clock. Two for the hour and two for the minutes, such as: for 9:00, punch in 0900. Select AM or PM on the screen. Set the date by pressing six numbers. Always press 0 in front of a one digit number. Press PROG to activate the clock. To clear a mistake when setting the clock, press CLEAR and begin again.

Record One Program and Watch Another
Put a tape in the VCR. Press the record button. After the recording begins, press the VCR button to turn off VCR. Select another channel on the TV.

Pause
The pause button may be used to interrupt tape recording or playback. To resume recording or playback, press the pause button again.

Channel Switching
Turn on the TV only. Select the first channel. Select a new channel by pressing the number of the second channel. If the channel has one digit, press 0 first.

Press PRV CH each time you want to change between these two channels.

Mute Button
Press the mute button to immediately turn the sound off. Press the mute button to turn the sound on again.

Name:

Take a Look

Follow the directions and answer the questions below using page 36.

1. Circle the button that fast-forwards a tape.

2. Underline the button that will begin a recording of a program.

3. Draw an X on the button that immediately turns the sound off.

4. Draw a star on the button that erases programming errors on the clock.

5. If you press PAUSE so a commercial isn't recorded, how do you start recording again?

_____

6. What numbers do you press to set the VCR clock for 4:30?

_____

7. After you have set the clock, how do you activate it?

_____

8. Write four important steps you must follow if you want to watch one program while you record another.

❶ _____

❷ _____

❸ _____

❹ _____

Survival Reading Skills EMC 573

Name:

Read to Eat

It's time for soup. All over the world, people gather up vegetables, meat, and grains, and toss them in a pot of boiling water. The result is a delicious lunch or dinner. The following ingredients are listed in recipes for Minestrone Soup.

Choose items from the list below to complete the Minestrone Soup recipe. Make sure your selections are sensible.

Ingredients for Minestrone Soup

parmesan cheese	coconut	ground beef
fish sticks	spaghetti	macaroni
stewed tomatoes	carrots	grape juice
water	apples	peaches in syrup
hot dogs	Italian seasoning	celery
zucchini	minced garlic	green beans
cinnamin	garbanzo beans	mustard

Minestrone Soup

1. Cook and stir _____ in the soup kettle until browned. Add a tablespoon of oil if needed. Drain the fat.

2. Add a cup each of diced _____ and _____.

3. Cook 5 minutes until vegetables are soft, stirring often.

4. Add liquids: _____; can of _____.

5. Bring to a boil, reduce heat and simmer 15 minutes.

6. Add 2 medium _____ ; squash (sliced); a can of beans, drained; and

   the pasta (_____ or _____).

7. Simmer until pasta is done.

8. Pour into bowls and sprinkle with _____.

Bon Appetit!

Name:

1

What's for Breakfast?

It's important to read the labels on the food you buy. Your favorite cereal may do somersaults when you pour on the milk, but it may not provide the nutrition you need.

The ingredients for two different cereals are shown below. Read the information and answer the questions about the two products on *What's for Breakfast?* ②.

Ingredient	Cereal A	Cereal B	Your Cereal
Calories	150	110	_____
Fat	1 gram	2 grams	_____
Cholesterol	0	0	_____
Sodium	140mg	110mg	_____
Carbohydrates	24g	30g	_____
Fiber	3g	1g	_____
Sugar	10g	14g	_____
Protein	3g	3g	_____

Percentage of Daily Food Values for a 2,000 Calorie a Day Diet

Ingredient	Cereal A	Cereal B	Your Cereal
Vitamin A	25	35	_____
Vitamin D	25	12	_____
Vitamin C	25	25	_____
Vitamin B_6	100	20	_____
Vitamin B_{12}	25	25	_____
Vitamin E	25	25	_____
Calcium	25	0	_____
Iron	100	25	_____
Potassium	2	0	_____
Copper	14	14	_____
Zinc	4	15	_____
Magnesium	100	20	_____
Phosphorus	15	15	_____
Riboflavin	15	20	_____
Folic Acid	25	10	_____
Thiamin	25	25	_____
Niacin	100	25	_____

Name:

What's for Breakfast?

2

1. Compare the two nutrition charts. In the percentage of Daily Food Values columns, which cereal has the greater number of high percentages?

_____

2. Some nutrients in Cereal B have a higher percentage than the same nutrients in Cereal A. List them.

_____   _____   _____

3. Which nutrients have the same percentage in both cereals?

_____   _____   _____

_____   _____   _____

4. Cereal A supplies 100 percent of several nutrients. Name them.

_____   _____

_____   _____

5. Cereal B has 0 percent of two nutrients. Name them.

_____   _____

6. Which cereal do you think provides the best nutrition? _____
Give at least three reasons for your choice.

_____

_____

_____

Homework
In the third column on the chart, fill in the information for a breakfast cereal from home. How does your cereal compare with the other two?

_____

_____

Name:

Lunchtime

On Saturday mornings, Nat runs errands for his mother and grandmother. He mows their lawns and does yard work for them. When it's 12:30, he stops for lunch. He spends some of the money he earns on lunch at the Snack Shack. Because he wants to try out for the swim team in the spring, he knows it's important to eat healthy foods.

On the back of the Snack Shack menu is a nutrition guide for the foods served in the restaurant. Nat read about the sandwiches before he placed his order.

Snack Shack — Hot Dogs — Hamburgers — Fries

	A	B	C	D	E	F	G	H	I
Super Cheeseburger	510	29	90	1100	28	10	4	15	25
Deluxe Cheeseburger	390	16	65	1040	24	9	12	12	25
Fish Sandwich	350	16	32	700	12	2	0	10	10
Chicken Supreme	250	3	45	500	22	3	8	10	15

Key

A - Calories
B - Grams of fat
C - Milligrams of cholesterol
D - Milligrams of Sodium
E - Grams of Protein
F - Vitamin A - percent of the daily nutrients needed
G- Vitamin C - percent of the daily nutrients needed
H - Calcium   - percent of the daily nutrients needed
I - Iron   - percent of the daily nutrients needed

Calories are the energy value of food. If you eat food with more calories than you use, you will gain weight.

The foods you eat should be low in fat, sodium, and cholesterol.

Name:

Lunchtime

2

Answer the following questions from the information on page 41.

1. Which sandwich has the fewest calories? _____

2. Which sandwich has the least salt (sodium)? _____

3. Which sandwich has the least amount of fat? _____

4. Which sandwich has the least cholesterol? _____

5. If you need 2,000 calories a day, how many Super Cheeseburgers can you eat

without going over 2,000 calories? _____

N at wasn't sure which sandwich he should order. The Super Cheeseburger had the most protein, but it had the most salt and fat. The Fish Sandwich had less fat, but it didn't have as much protein. Nat decided to use a system of points to decide which sandwich was the best one to eat. He added points for cholesterol, calories, salt, and fat. He subtracted points for the nutrients that his body needed. The sandwich with the lowest points was the one he would order.

Predict which sandwich Nat will order. _____

Nat's Point System

1. Add 5 points for each 50 calories.
2. Add 5 points for each 10 grams of fat.
3. Add 5 points for each 10 mg of cholesterol.
4. Add 5 points for each 100 mg of sodium.
5. Subtract 5 points for each 5 grams of protein.

6. Subtract the percentage of vitamin A.
7. Subtract the percentage of vitamin C.
8. Subtract 5 points for each 10% of calcium.
9. Subtract 5 points of each 10% of iron.

Nat did not round off the numbers to the nearest 10, 50, or 100. Twenty-four grams of fat, for example, earned 5 points for each 10 grams (2 x 5). The 4 wasn't counted.

Tally the score for each sandwich listed below.

Super Cheeseburger $50 + 10 + 45 + 55 - 25 - 10 - 4 - 5 - 10 = 106$

Deluxe Cheeseburger _____

Fish Sandwich _____

Chicken Supreme _____

Which sandwich did Nat decide to buy? _____

Name: _____

Aisle Search

Beth's family moved from their apartment to a new house. They needed to build a fence around their yard so they could adopt a dog. While Beth's parents bought the lumber and cement, Beth looked for the other supplies they needed. A sign in the store listed the kinds of merchandise found in each aisle. The aisles were numbered.

Aisle Numbers

Building Tools	Aisle 6
Lighting	Aisle 2
Hardware for Gates	Aisle 3
Paints and Stains	Aisle 12
Plants	Aisle 10
Electrical Supplies	Aisle 15
Nails, Screws, Bolts, Building Hardware	Aisle 4
Plumbing Supplies	Aisle 1
Protective Clothing	Aisle 11
Fireplace Supplies	Aisle 7
Step Stools and Ladders	Aisle 5
Garden Supplies	Aisle 9

Write the aisle number for each item on Beth's list.

two hammers _____

drill and drill bits _____

ladder _____

waterproof stain for the wood _____

pliers _____

nails, screws, bolts _____

a hand saw _____

a tool box _____

3 pair of gloves _____

hinges and a lock for the gate _____

Reading for Details

Chapter Introduction

Reading for details involves pulling out relevant information from the text. This skill is important in planning "construction" projects and in making purchasing decisions.

The following pages contain projects that help students practice this important skill. They will read instructions, plan a garden, and find out the importance of reading when buying a product.

Note: The paper boat in the activity on pages 45 and 46 is not easily constructed from paper. This activity is intended to practice reading for details, not as an actual "make-it" project.

Extension Activity

Before working on Gardening from January to December—bring in books and pictures of gardens, both flower and fruit and vegetable. If you are able, bring in samples of some of the plants mentioned. You might even want to start a mini-garden in milk cartons that the students can take home to transplant in their own yards. Vocabulary: harvest, bloom, trellis.

Name:

Make a Paper Boat

Marta wanted to make a paper boat for a construction contest at school. Before she could build the boat, she had to read the directions to find out what supplies she would need.

Read the directions for Marta's paper boat. List all the needed materials in the space provided on Make a Paper Boat 2. Then follow the remaining directions on sheet 2.

Make a pattern

1. Cut two rectangles 20 cm long and 8 cm wide for the bottom and top.

2. Mark the center point on one short side of both bottom and top rectangles.

3. Measure back 6 cm on both long sides. Make marks. Using a ruler and pencil, connect each of these marks.

4. The sail is an 8 x 10 cm rectangle cut from corner to corner.

5. For the 2 sides and the front, cut three pices that measure 14 x 5 cm.

6. The back piece is a 8 x 10 rectangle.

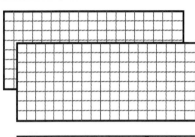

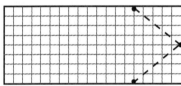

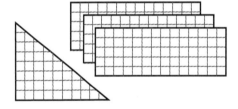

Using the pieces you cut, follow these directions.

1. Cut a 6 cm long, 4 cm wide rectangle from the center of the top deck of the boat.

2. Tape all the patterns except the sail to lightweight cardboard or posterboard. Cut out the pieces.

3. Decorate the pieces using felt pens or crayons. Give your boat a name.

4. Tape all the pieces together. Fold one side piece to fit around the pointed bow.

5. Use the sharp end of a wooden skewer to poke a mast hole into the deck.

6. Glue the sail to the skewer and insert the "mast" through the hole.

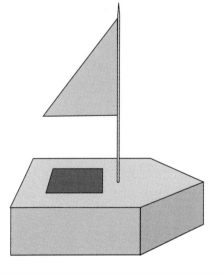

Name:

2

Make a Paper Boat

List all the materials that Marta needs here:

_____   _____

_____   _____

_____   _____

_____   _____

_____   _____

_____   _____

**Marta looked in her craft box.
This is what she saw.**

**Help Marta make a shopping list so that
she will have all the necessary materials.**

Shopping List

_____

_____

_____

_____

_____

_____

_____

_____

Name:

Gardening from January to December

Arnold lives in a mild California climate area near San Francisco Bay. His parents gave him a sunny area to plant a garden. He can choose what he would like to grow. Arnold wants to have flowers and vegetables growing all the months of the year. He plans to have the tall plants near the fence and the smaller plants in the front so all the plants have sun. He looked up plants in the garden book and made a list of plants he wanted to raise. He wrote down the size of the plants, when he should plant them, and when they would bloom or grow fruits and vegetables.

Flowers

Gladiolus   Blooms from spring to fall. Grows 18-24 inches high. Plant in October and November.

Daffodil   Plant early to late fall. Many kinds and sizes. Blooms in spring.

Tulip   Blooms in the spring. Grows 10-12 inches. Plant in the fall.

Snapdragon   Plant in September. Blooms in winter through spring. Grows 6 inches to 4 feet.

Forget-Me-Not   Blooms in the late spring through fall. Grows 6 to 12 inches. Plant in the spring or fall.

African Daisy   12 to 18 inches high. Blooms late fall to early spring.

Wallflower   1 to 2-1/2 feet tall. Blooms from February to May. Plant in the spring.

Chrysanthemum   2 to 3 feet high. Blooms June to late summer. Plant in spring.

Shasta Daisy   Grows 1 to 3 feet. Same bloom cycle as the chrysanthemum.

Common Sneeze-Weed   Blooms August and September. 6 feet tall.

Perennial Pincushion   Blooms from May through December. Grows to 2-1/2 feet. Plant in the fall.

Gardening from January to December

Larkspur 3 to 4 feet tall. Blooms in spring. Plant in fall and winter.

Common Sunflower 7 to 10 feet tall. Plant in spring. Blooms summer and fall.

Zinnia 1/2 to 3 feet. Plant when weather is warm. Blooms summer and fall.

Fruits and Vegetables

Lettuce Under one foot. Plant in late summer for winter harvest. Plant in October for spring harvest.

Cabbage 12 to 18 inches high. Plant in January and February for spring harvest. Plant in July for late fall harvest.

Tomatoes 2 to 4 feet. Ripens in late summer and fall. Plant in the spring.

Corn Very tall, 6 to 8 feet. Plant in spring and harvest in fall.

Asparagus Under one foot. Harvest in the spring. New plants every ten years. Plant midwinter.

Broccoli 1 to 2 feet. Cool weather vegetable.

Pumpkins 1-1/2 to 2 feet. Plant in the spring. Harvest in the fall.

Carrots Tops grow 9-12 inches. Grows during the cool season.

Peas Plant in the fall or winter. Harvest in winter or spring. Needs trellis or 3-foot wire nets to climb.

String beans Grows during summer months. Plant in the spring. Grows 3 feet high.

Name: _____

Gardening from January to December

Use the information from pages 47 and 48 to fill in the chart. List the name of each plant, its size, and when it blooms or produces food.

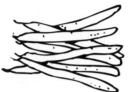 Arnold's Garden

Name of the Plant	Size	Bloom/Fruit Time

Name:

Gardening from January to December

What will be blooming or fruiting in Arnold's garden each season? Choose plants from the chart. Remember, the tall plants should be closest to the fence. Write the names of the plants you choose on the garden plans. Include at least five plants for each season.

winter

spring

summer

fall

Name: _____

Read Carefully!

1

Samantha ordered a new backpack from a catalog. She carried a heavy load of books home from school each day. She needed a large, sturdy backpack. She looked at the pictures in the advertisement and saw one that looked just right. Her choice is circled. After the first week, the straps broke. The company wouldn't refund her money.

Backpacks Galore!

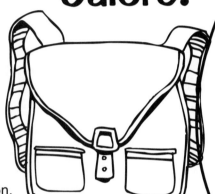

A16

All Purpose.
Blue, red, or green.
Safety pouch inside
main compartment.
Weather resistant nylon.
Holds up to 25 pounds.
Padded shoulder straps.

A 17

School Daze Brand. Olive or tan.
Large compartment and one
outside pouch. Reinforced
shoulder straps. Padded for
shoulder comfort. Holds up to six
pounds.

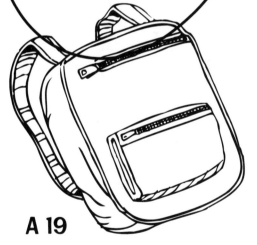

A 18

Aluminum frame overnighter
backpack. Side pocket
for water bottle. Detachable
pouch. Extra strength straps.
Waist belt. Strap for sleeping
bag.

A 19

Women's lightweight pack. All-
weather coated nylon. Side and
back pockets. Large capacity.
Padded extra-strength curved
shoulder straps. Water bottle
strap.

Reading for Details

Read Carefully!

2

Answer the following questions about Samantha's backpack described on page 51.

1. If Samantha had read the description of the backpack carefully, she would not have ordered it. What clues in the advertisement show that it wasn't the right backpack for her?

   _____

2. Why do you think the company wouldn't refund Samantha's money?

   _____

3. If Alice wanted to order a backpack for a daytime hiking trip to the state park, which

   one should she order? _____

   Why? _____

4. Omar wanted a backpack for a three-day trip in Yosemite National Park. Which

   backpack should he order?_____

   Why? _____

Now it's your turn. Using your own backpack or a friend's, write an advertisement that a store might use to try to sell it. Be sure to include its brand, what it is made from, and any special features that make it useful. Include an illustration.

   _____

   _____

   _____

   _____

   _____

   _____

Visualizing What You Read

Chapter Introduction

Visualizing when you read is a very important component of comprehension. The clearer the students can "see" what they are reading, the better able they are to understand.

In this section of Survival Reading Skills, students are asked to visualize the words they are reading and turn them into pictures.

For *Drawing a Map,* one-inch graph paper would be very helpful for students who have a difficult time planning.

Extension Activities

📖 Have students write directions from their houses to a nearby store, friend's house, a park, or a mailbox. Exchange paragraphs with a classmate. Have students draw maps from the directions they receive. Compare the results. Were the written directions clear?

📖 Have your students draw a map from their school to their house, adding as much detail as possible.

📖 Give students a piece of drawing paper. Give them oral directions for drawing a simple picture that you hold in your hand so that they cannot see it. When finished, have the students hold up their pictures to share. See how each of us visualizes differently.

Survival Reading Skills EMC 573

Name: _____

Drawing a Map

Maggie plans to walk to Julia's house Saturday afternoon to work on a science project. On Friday, Julia gave her written directions from the school to her house. Maggie decided to draw a map from the directions. She thought it would be easier to follow the map when she walked to Julia's house.

Read the directions Julia gave to Maggie. Draw a map showing the route from Washington School to Julia's house. Label the streets. Use symbols for the stores, the post office, and the stop sign. You may invent your own symbols. Add a legend to the bottom of your map to explain what the symbols mean. For example, you might write an S where the stop sign is or draw a stamped envelope to represent the post office.

The Directions to Julia's House

- Walk to the corner of Elm and Walnut to Washington School.
- Cross the street and walk three blocks North on Walnut Street.
- Turn to the right on Cedar Street.
- Walk two blocks past Food Land, Video Center, the post office, and the park.
- Turn right at the stop sign on to Peach Tree Lane.
- Walk one block to Plum Court, which is on the right side of the street.
- My house number is 691. It's the second house on the left side of the court.

Legend

Ⓧ Washington School

Food Land

Video Center

Post Office

park

stop sign

Julia's House

Elm Street

Ⓧ

Name:

Picture This

Read the following description and draw a picture that shows what you read using very exact measurements. You will need a ruler, pencil, and paper to complete the drawing.

Directions:

1. Find the middle of Side A. Put a dot there.

2. Extend Side A 1/2 inch to the left.

3. Using a ruler, connect the end of the 1/2 inch line to the left end of Side B.

4. Measure up 3" from the dot in the middle of Side A. Make another dot.

5. Connect the two dots with a straight line.

6. Draw a triangle using the line in Step 5 as one side of the triangle and the left side of Side A as the second side. Draw the third side of the triangle connecting the two lines.

7. Form a second triangle. The right side of Side A and the line in Step 5 are two of the sides. Draw the third side to connect the two sides.

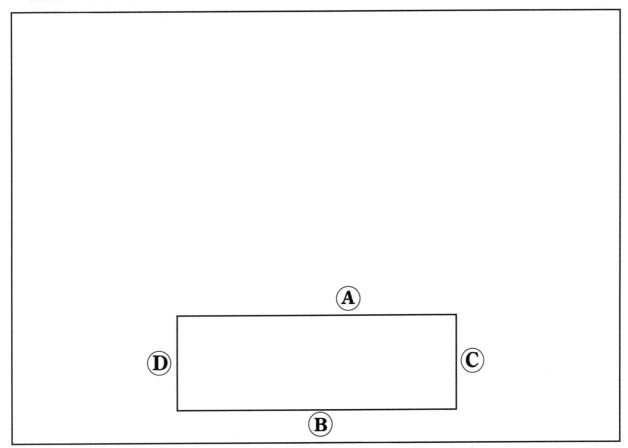

Draw your own picture using a ruler and very exact measurements. Write a description and give to someone. See if the person can duplicate your picture. Good luck!

Sequencing and Schedules

In this section of *Survival Reading Skills*, students will practice these important skills by reading about a famous American, then sequence the important events in his life. They will also make choices for packing items depending on a schedule.

For the *Benjamin Franklin* time line, you can use adding machine tape. Each student can draw a long time line and mark one year every two inches. The time line boxes can be glued right on the tape. In this way, the time relationship of events is easily seen.

Discuss the term "chronological." Ask students to list important events in their lives in chronological order.

When you read an interesting story, the writer doesn't always begin with the event that happened first. For example, John visited the Grand Canyon in August. When he told his class about his trip, he described what he saw at the Grand Canyon first. Then he talked about traveling on the train to Arizona and getting ready for the trip.

Read this biography about a famous American. The events in the story are not necessarily in chronological order. You will then follow instructions on sheets 2 and 3 to complete a time line of Franklin's life.

Benjamin Franklin

Benjamin Franklin was a great inventor. When he was 77, he invented bifocal glasses so he could read books and see objects that were far away without changing glasses. When he was 35, he invented the Franklin Stove so people could have heat from a wood-burning stove in the center of the room. His experiments with electricity from 1747 to 1752 led to the invention of the lightning rod.

Franklin enjoyed writing. He published his own newspaper, *The Pennsylvania Gazette,* when he was 23. He started the first public library in the American colonies and published *Poor Richard's Almanack* when he was 25. Franklin became interested in newspapers when he was 12. He was sent to live with his older brother, James, to learn about printing newspapers. When he was 16, he secretly wrote humorous stories for his brother's newspaper.

Franklin worked to improve the lives of people who lived in the colonies. When he was 47, he organized a better mail-delivery system. He petitioned Congress to end slavery in 1789.

Franklin was well-known in England and France. In 1757, he went to England to gain more freedom for the people living in America. When he was 60, he convinced the British Parliament to end the Stamp Act, which added taxes to printed documents and materials bought by the colonists.

During the American Revolutionary War, when Franklin was 70 years old, he became minister to France. The French helped the colonists win their freedom from England. Six years later, at the end of the war with England, Franklin helped write the peace treaty. He had also been one of the signers of the Declaration of Independence in 1776. He was an important member of the Constitutional Convention in Philadelphia when he was 81 years old.

Benjamin Franklin died in Philadelphia in 1790 when he was 84 years old.

Name: _____

Benjamin Franklin

On each of the 15 lines below, write a few words about something Benjamin Franklin did, or list an event in his life. Write a date in each of the boxes. The date of his birth has been given in the first box. To arrive at this date, Franklin's age (84) was subtracted from the year he died (1790). If Franklin's age is given instead of the year of the event, add his age at that time to 1706, his birthdate.

Example: he was 70 years old when he became minister to
France. Add 70 to 1706. He became minister to France in 1776.

Benjamin Franklin was born.	1706
Started first public library. Published Poor Richard's Almanack.	1731
Petitioned Congress to end slavery.	1789

Transfer the information to the boxes on the next page. Cut out the boxes. Arrange them in chronological order and glue them on a large piece of paper. Write Benjamin Franklin's name at the top of the page. Illustrate your time line.

Sequencing and Schedules

Name:

Benjamin Franklin

3

1706	**1731**	**1789**
Benjamin Franklin was born.	Started first public library. Published Poor Richard's Almanac.	Petitioned Congress to end slavery.

Name:

An Invitation

May and Joshua received an invitation from their aunt for a weekend at the beach.

Surf and Sand Weekend

The fun begins at 3:30 on Friday, May 14. Be ready! It's a three-hour drive to Sandy Cove. We'll feast at our favorite fast-food restaurant on the way. After you unpack, it's off to the beach for a marshmallow roast and a look at the stars.

Saturday	7:00 A. M.	Breakfast
	7:45	Head for the beach to see what we can find
	10:00	Back to the house to check out our treasures
	11:00	Lunch
	12:00	Downtown to the Ice Cream Shoppe for dessert and saltwater taffy. A tour of the souvenir stores.
	1:30	Beach Hike (4 miles round trip). We'll check out the tidepools, see what we can see with the binoculars, and stop at the aquarium for a look at the fish.
	5:00	We're home in time for dinner.
	6:30	We'll walk to the beach and watch the sun sink into the ocean.
	8:00	We'll munch on cookies and play your favorite board games until you fall asleep.

Sunday we'll drive back early in the morning so you can rest up for school.

Love,

Aunt Susan

P.S. I already checked with your mom, and she said you could go.

Name:

An Invitation

Joshua and May had to pack their bags on Thursday. They packed up their socks, PJs, and their underwear. What else should they take to the beach?

Read the invitation again. Use the activities their aunt mentions to decide what else they should pack. Write at least ten items on the lines below.

Aunt Susan's favorite cookies

toothbrush and toothpaste

Answer Key

The Science Fair - Page 3

A. Evaporation. The heat from the sun causes water to evaporate faster.
B. Water tension. (No conclusion given.)
C. (No title given. No conclusion given.)
Best answers are:
    Omar -   1
    Donna - 2
    Sally -   3

Track and Field - Page 4

100 Yard Dash	High Jump	
Place	Number	Place
5	8	1
4	30	2
2	18	6
3	19	3
1	20	5
6	39	4

Track and Field - Page 5

Pole Vault		Shot Put		
Number	Place	Number	School	Place
25	1	19	Taylor	1
18	2	11	Taylor	3
15	3	46	Anderson	6
22	4	20	Anderson	2
10	5	28	Taylor	5
12	5	15	Anderson	4

Track and Field - Page 6

Anderson High School

1st place wins:	1	1st place points:	5
2nd place wins:	3	2nd place points:	9
3rd place wins:	0	3rd place points:	0
		total points:	14

Taylor High School

1st place wins:	3	1st place points:	15
2nd place wins:	1	2nd place points:	3
3rd place wins:	4	3rd place points:	4
		total points:	22

1. Taylor, by 8 points
2. Anderson: Washington, Fernandes, Nguyen
   Taylor: Rashad, Brenner
3. Washington, 8
4. Answers will vary.

In-Line Skates - Page 10

Best Buy Catalog

Name: First	Middle Initial	Last	Area Code	Telephone
Jeffrey	A.	O'Brien	(523)	787-3344

Address	City	State	Zip Code
44 Washington Ave.	Oakville	CA	97655

	Item	Catalog Number	Weight	Size	Color	Price
1	Protective Pack	L69398	2.2 lbs.	---	---	$18.69
2	Dial-a-Size Helmet	M89356	2.8 lbs.	---	will vary	$41.20
3	Lightning Skates	C97321	8 lbs.	---	---	$51.98
4						

Total price of order:	$111.87
Sales tax (8%):	$8.95
Total weight: 13.16 Shipping and handling:	$12.50
Amount owed:	$133.32

In Line Skates - Page 11

1. He received two protective packs. There was a protective pack that came with the skates he ordered and one set he ordered separately.
2. He could return the protective pack he ordered and keep the one that came with the skates.
3. Jeffrey's refund would be $23.88. $18.69 + $1.50 + $3.69 Cost of the merchandise x .08 sales tax + $3.69 for postage. Since the shipping charge is the same for all orders between 10 and 19.9 pounds, Jeffrey would not receive a refund for shipping and handling.
4. About 30 days.
5. Read the description better.
6. Answers will vary.

Put It Together - Page 13

1. Read directions.
   Make sure all parts listed are in the package.
   See what tools you will need.
   Set up a tool box.
2. Wood glue, screwdriver, towel, hammer
3. back, 2 sides, 3 shelves, 12 wooden pegs, 18 screws

Page 14

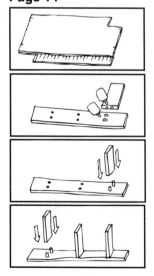

Page 15

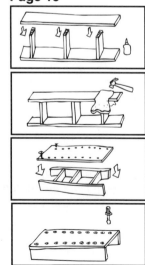

Survival Reading Skills EMC 573

Answer Key

Just For Fun - page 16
If you wish to move a mountain, carry away a few stones at a time.

Knot Work - page 18
1. B   2. D   3. F   4. A   5. E   6. G   7. C

School Store - page 21
1. 3 months
2. 1 day
3. Another student will substitute.
4. Sell, put away merchandise, keep records, make up missed class work.
5. 40 minutes
6. Answers will vary, but may include: use good manners, be polite, make suggestions, smile.
7. $2.40

Camp Goodtimes - page 25
1. Section 3
2. So organizations can't discriminate against people.
3. Parent must notify if someone else is picking up a camper.
   Photo I.D. for people picking up camper
   Emergency phone numbers
   Medications listed
   Allergies and health information listed
   List of any activities camper can't take part in
4. To make sure the camper stays healthy and safe.
5. Parent or guardian
6. May 1

Applying for a Job - page 27
Errors on application:
1. Name listed in the wrong order
2. Left out the name of the state
3. Had not graduated when he turned in the application
4. He will be a college student in the fall.
5. He mixed up previous work experience and job he would like to have
6. He needs to explain that he wants full-time work in the summer and weekends in the fall.
7. He can't work without a permit until July 1.

1. After July 1
2. Palma, Martin Antonio
3. Answers will vary.
4. I would like to work full time during the summer, and one day a weekend starting in the fall.

The Winning Ticket - page 31
1. March 1
2. No
3. Fill out the information at the bottom of the entry blank, turn it in at the counter, and rent a movie.
4. Hundreds
5. Answers will vary.
6. A free candy bar with your next movie rental

Rebate - page 32
1. Proof-of-purchase seals from 5 boxes
   Entry blank on the back of the box
   Register receipts
2. You have to subtract the cost of the postage from the amount of the rebate. You could lose money.
3. By July 20
4. Eight weeks after July 20

Buy! Buy! Buy! - page 34
Fluffy - 3
Sam's Pizza - 4
Sneakers - 1
Glow Toothpaste - 2

Take a Look - page 37
Marked diagram of remote control for (1-4)

5. Press the pause button again.
6. "0430"
7. Press the PROG button
8. Put in the tape, press RECORD, press the VCR button to turn it off. Select a channel on TV.

Read to Eat - page 38
1. ground beef
2. carrots, celery
4. water, stewed tomatoes
6. zucchini, spaghetti, macaroni
8. parmesan cheese

What's for Breakfast? - page 40
1. Cereal A
2. Vitamin A, zinc, riboflavin
3. Vitamins E, B_{12}, C, thiamin, phosphorus, copper
4. Vitamin B_6, niacin, magnesium, iron
5. potassium, calcium
6. Answers will vary. Students should name cereal A because it is lower in fat and sugar, higher in fiber, and has a higher vitamin and mineral content.

Answer Key

Lunchtime - page 42
1. Chicken Supreme
2. Chicken Supreme
3. Chicken Supreme
4. Fish Sandwich
5. 3 Super Cheeseburgers

1. Super Cheeseburger	106
2. Deluxe Cheeseburger	64
3. Fish Sandwich	68
4. Chicken Sandwich	29

He bought the Chicken Sandwich.

Aisle Search - page 44
6, 6, 5, 12, 6, 4, 6, 6, 11 or 9, 3

Make a Paper Boat - page 46
Materials needed:
centimeter graph paper, ruler, pencil, scissors, cardboard or posterboard, felt pen or crayons, tape, glue, wooden skewers, construction paper.
Shopping list:
centimeter graph paper
cardboard or posterboard
felt pens or crayons
wooden skewers
construction paper

Gardening from January to December - page 49

Name of Plant	Size	Bloom or Harvest Time
Gladiolus	18–24"	Spring–Fall
Daffodils	varies	Spring
Tulips	10–12"	Spring
Snapdragons	6"–4 ft.	Winter–Spring
Forget-Me-Not	6–12"	Late Spring–Fall
African Daisy	12–18"	Late Fall–Early Spring
Wallflower	1–2 1/2 ft.	Feb.–May
Chrysanthemum	2–3 ft.	June–Late Summer
Shasta Daisy	1–3 ft.	June–Late Summer
Sneeze-Weed	6 ft.	August and September
Pincushion	2 1/2 ft.	May–December
Larkspur	3–4 ft.	Spring
Sunflower	7–10 ft.	Summer, Fall
Zinnia	1/2–3 ft.	Summer, Fall
lettuce	Under 1 ft.	Winter, Spring
cabbage	12–18"	Spring, Late Fall
tomatoes	2–4 ft.	Summer, Fall
corn	6–8 ft.	Fall
asparagus	Under 1 ft.	Spring
broccoli	1–2 ft.	Winter
pumpkins	1 1/2–2 ft.	Fall
carrots	tops 9–12"	cool season
peas	3 ft.	Winter, Spring
string beans	3 ft.	Summer

Gardening from January to December - page 50
Choices will vary. Let students evaluate each other's responses.

Read Carefully! - page 52
1. The information said she carries a heavy load of books. The advertisement states it holds up to only 6 pounds.
2. The load of books was too heavy for the bag.
3. A19 - all weather, padded, water bottle strap
4. A18 - overnighter backpack, extra strength straps, strap for sleeping bag

Drawing a Map - page 54
Symbols will vary.

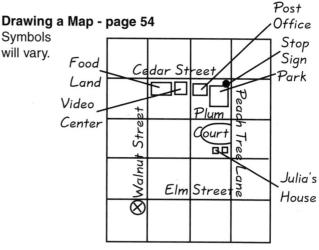

Picture This - page 55

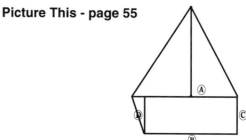

Benjamin Franklin - page 58
Possible events and dates:

Became interested in newspapers	1718
Wrote funny stories for brother's newspaper	1722
Published *Pennsylvania Gazette*	1729
Invented the Franklin Stove	1741
Experimented with electricity	1747–1752
Organized a better mail delivery system	1753
Went to England to work for freedom for colonies	1757
Convinced England to end the Stamp Act	1766
Signed Declaration of Independence	1776
Became minister to France	1776
Helped write peace treaty with England	1782
Invented bifocal glasses	1783
Member of Constitutional Convention	1787
Died in Philadelphia	1790

An Invitation - page 61
Accept any reasonable answers. Possible items may include: swimming suit, walking shoes, board games, binoculars, camera, beach towel, marshmallow roasting sticks, marshmallows, sunglasses, reef shoes, shorts, sunscreen, day pack, hat, jacket, bucket to collect things, spending money.